The Mulberry Harbour Project In Wigtownshire 1942 - 1944
by
A. T. Murchie

Local History Series No 4

Copyright
A. T. Murchie 1993
2nd Edition 1999

ISBN 1 872350 62 3

Published by G.C. Book Publishers Ltd
17 North Main Street
Wigtown, Newton Stewart,
Scotland DG8 9HL

Tel/fax 01988 40 2499
email: sales@gcbooks.demon.co.uk
website: http//www.gcbooks.demon.co.uk

CONTENTS

List of Illustrations

			Page
Chapter	1	....	5
	2	....	21
	3	....	49
	4	....	56
	5	....	58

Glossary of terms 60

Acknowledgments 63

The Mulberry Harbour Project

Aerial photograph of Mulberry B at Arromanches taken on 9 September 1944. In the foreground several large vessels lying inshore of Phoenix Breakwater. On the right 2000ft Swiss Roll used by Royal Navy. Spud Pontoons with floating piers centre and left.

IWM BV1020

In Wigtownshire 1942 -1944

THE MULBERRY HARBOUR

Chapter 1

In Spring 1941 after eighteen months of war the greater part of Europe was in enemy hands. An assault on Europe seemed likely to be a long way ahead but planning for a "Second Front" had already commenced. Allied strategy required that operations in the Mediterranean theatre take precedence during 1942 but preparation for an assault across the English Channel did not cease. A major part of the planning concerned the means of landing and maintaining a large force under hostile conditions. When landings were made in North Africa and in Italy the ports were virtually undefended and were quickly brought back into full working order. In contrast an Allied raid on Dieppe in August 1942 when almost 3000 men were killed or captured showed that German forces would defend and, if necessary, destroy ports to prevent their use by an invading force. Field Marshal Rommel had constructed strong defences on all likely invasion beaches in Northern France, Belgium and Holland and he clearly hoped to rapidly repel any attack.

The planners concluded that in order to provide the anticipated massive requirement to discharge men, vehicles, ammunition, fuel and other supplies it would be essential to provide berthing facilities in sheltered water. What was required was an artificial harbour which could be pre-fabricated then taken across the Channel for installation on the chosen landing beach. This would have to be designed, tested then built in a very limited period of time.

The Mulberry Harbour Project

Six span floating pier at Cairnhead ready to receive Spud Pontoon. 20 April 1943
IWM H29426

In Wigtownshire 1942 -1944

In July 1917 during World War I Britain was considering an attack on the islands of Borkum and Sylt in the Friesian Islands off the German coast. Winston Churchill, then a member of the War Cabinet, suggested to Prime Minister Lloyd George that "a number of flat bottomed barges made of concrete could be towed across, then sunk to form a torpedo and weather proof harbour, like an atoll, in the open sea." His remarkable foresight then was now renewed as he urged the planners to look again at the concept of a floating harbour.

Early in 1941 the War Office Directorate of Transportation formed a branch named Transportation 5, or TN5, with responsibility for port engineering. In charge of this section was Major Bruce White, a widely experienced and highly qualified civil engineer who had specialised in development of transport systems. He had built up a team of civil and port engineers for TN5 before early in 1942 the Admiralty, who considered harbours to be their province, reluctantly agreed that TN5 be given responsibility for the planning, testing and construction of invasion harbours. For security purposes the invasion harbour project had been given the codename *Mulberry*, an apparently fortuitous choice.

Prime Minister Churchill's clear concept of the problems involved is illustrated in a directive which he wrote on 30th May, 1942 to Admiral Mountbatten who had recently been appointed to command Combined Operations. On the following report about piers which had been submitted to him Churchill wrote "They must float up and down on the tide. The anchor problem must be mastered. The ships must have a side-flap cut in them and a drawbridge large enough to over reach the

The Mulberry Harbour Project

Line of vehicles coming ashore from pierhead. August 1943

IWM H30930

moorings of the piers. Let me have the best solution worked out. Don't argue the matter. The difficulties will argue for themselves!"

Piers for use on Beaches.

CONDITIONS OF BEACH

1. Average gradient is 1 in 200 and beaches are open to the south west.

CONDITIONS OF TIDE

2. Range of spring tides is 30 feet and the strength of the tide parallel to the beach is 4 knots at springs. (Spring tides. Higher than normal tides which coincide with full and new moons.)

SCAFFOLDING PIERS

3. A pier to be of use for unloading ships of 20 foot draught would have to be 1 mile in length and 40 foot in height at the seaward end. The present type of scaffolding pier does not exceed 20 foot in height. It is doubtful whether a pier of these large dimensions could be made with scaffolding, but in any case the amount of material required would be prohibitive.

The Mulberry Harbour Project

LST 13 arriving at Spud Pontoon. August 1943

IWM H31628

In Wigtownshire 1942 -1944

PONTOON PIERS

4. A pontoon pier would have to be similar in length. All floating piers suffer from the disadvantage of having to be securely moored with heavy anchors. Even then they are most vulnerable and will not stand up to a gale of wind. The strength of the tide is so great that the moorings will have to be very large. If large pontoons were moored, 20 yards apart, at least 200 anchors would be required. The sea-ward end of a floating pier must be particularly well moored and the mooring chains form an obstacle to ships coming alongside. Owing to the poor ratio between the weight of a floating pontoon and the weight they can carry, and to their vulnerability to sea, wind and tide, they are not favoured in comparison with scaffolding piers on open beaches.

In the autumn of 1942 TN5 received from Combined Operations Headquarters a *Mulberry* specification which required "a pierhead capable of berthing three 2000 ton vessels simultaneously and a pier which would allow continuous traffic flow over a length of not less than one mile."

From a number of schemes received and evaluated it was decided to carry out full scale trials on three to decide which was most suitable. First was a fixed pier and pierhead designed by a Consulting Engineer, Iorys Hughes. Second came a floating roadway which was the invention of Ronald Hamilton and, finally, a design for a floating bridge and pierhead conceived by TN5 engineers.

In January 1943 TN5 formed a Royal Engineer unit which was given the cumbersome title

The Mulberry Harbour Project

Hippo No. 1 placed at the end of Garlieston Harbour. 60 ton floating crane moored alongside. 30th October, 1943.

In Wigtownshire 1942 -1944

'No.1 Transportation Fixed and Floating Equipment Development and Training Depot' which was placed under the command of Major J.G. Carline, a professional engineer who in pre-war days had worked for Assam Railways. This unit now became responsible for development of, and training in the use of, *Mulberry* Piers. A first requirement was a suitable development area. A search around the coastline found that the Solway tides provided conditions very similar to those prevailing on the likely invasion beaches on the Normandy coastline. A stretch of coast on the west side of Wigtown Bay seemed suitable, there were beaches with reasonable access; the area was sufficently remote for security purposes; the harbour at Garlieston was available to bring in equipment; the Bay was not already in other military use - nearby Luce Bay could not have been used because of existing bombing and gunnery ranges. Local reconnaissance soon confirmed these conditions and a site was selected to construct a camp at Cairnhead close to Isle of Whithorn village.

The War Diary of 933 Port Construction and Repair Company, Royal Engineers, records that they moved from Garelochhead on the Clyde to Cairnhead in mid-February 1943 then, on 4th March, 1943, that "Camp for 120 men with Nissen hut accommodation complete with Mess Rooms, Officers and Sergeants Mess and ancillary buildings which was commenced on 12th February was completed today." Major Carline now established his Headquarters at this Camp.

167 Railway Bridging Company, Royal Engineers based at Barrow-in-Furness had been involved for several weeks on "Bridge Erections Trials" when on 21st February, 1943 their Commanding Officer, Major J.D. Watson, issued an Operation Order which instructed cessation of

The Mulberry Harbour Project

Tug *Ebro* towing pontoon section.

IWM H36517

In Wigtownshire 1942 -1944

work at Barrow as it was now intended to "erect a complete bridge of 5 or 6 spans in the open sea at a site in Wigtown Bay as soon as all necessary materials arrive there." The order added that TN5 would arrange Royal Navy tank landing craft to move materials including 28 two and three ton concrete mooring blocks, steel bridge spans and various other bridging materials. Materials of less bulk would be despatched by rail. The order also specified that "TN5 are arranging for a 60 ton floating crane and two tugs for use at the erection site."

The War Diary of 167 Company subsequently records that No.3 Section under the command of Captain D.J. Tonks moved to Cairnhead between 1st March and 19th March. Progress Reports show that three tank landing craft, No's 238, 270 and 273, duly arrived in Barrow then, after loading, "Left Ramsden Dock, Barrow en route for Douglas, Isle of Man then Garlieston at 0900 hours on Friday 5 March 1943." The reason for the indirect route via Douglas is not explained but was probably due to wartime movement restrictions. Two tank landing craft made another return journey to bring the remainder of the equipment into Garlieston on 21st March, 1943. Several reinforced concrete pontoons were towed from Barrow, the tug *Abeille* left Barrow with two pontoons on 2nd March and the tug *Ebro* towed two pontoons arriving in Garlieston on 21st March.

The *Ebro*, a Dutch vessel now under control of the Ministry of War Transport, was to remain in Garlieston, with Captain Jansma and his Dutch crew for the remainder of the *Mulberry* exercise. The other tug allocated by the M.O.W.T. was the *Ajay*, a small river tug from the Thames, with her civilian crew of two brothers. Her normal task of towing barges between the docks in the Isle of

The Mulberry Harbour Project

Bridge spans being placed on Beetles by 60 ton floating crane prior to towing to Cairnhead. April 1943

IWM H29382

Dogs and up-river warehouses had ended when wartime restrictions meant the closure of the London Docks.

933 Company War Diary records that on 24th February "Warrant Officer Humphries was supplied as Chief Engineer to MOWT 50 ton Floating Crane" inferring that the crane was then in Garlieston.

In addition to those based at Cairnhead Camp some 20 Sappers were accommodated in the village hall in Garlieston which had been requisitioned. This ensured that men were readily available to meet the demands of operations in a tidal harbour. One unhappy Sapper is reputed to have been overheard in the bar of the Grapes Hotel in Whithorn complaining that "high tide at Garlieston is always at three o'clock in the morning." Clearly he was not aware of the work of the University of Liverpool Tidal Institute and Observatory, though possibly their tidal predictions were not published during the war years!

Some of the men based in Garlieston were involved in maintaining security which was strictly enforced. Garlieston Bay and the coastline down to Isle of Whithorn was 'out of bounds' to local fishermen though it appears that an occasional lobster or box of freshly caught fish arriving in the kitchens at Cairnhead ensured that this was not too strictly enforced. The public road passing close to the sea at Cairnhead and the footpaths around Garlieston Bay and Rigg Bay were regularly patrolled by military motor cycles. It has been reported, though not in an official publication, that

The Mulberry Harbour Project

l to r Major J. G. Carline; Major General Sir Riddle Webster, Quartermaster General; Brigadier Bruce White and Major Stirling. Garlieston Harbour 13th March, 1943.

iwm

In Wigtownshire 1942 -1944

MI5 sent an Officer to test security. He was said to have walked all over the area dressed as a tramp, even visiting the bar of the Galloway Arms Hotel in Garlieston when an off-duty Major Carline was having a drink with visiting U.S. Army Officers. The veracity of this story must be in some doubt. In 1943 Garlieston, together with nearby Wigtown and Whithorn, had a resident policeman of the wholly local Wigtownshire Constabulary. A tramp not already known who suddenly appeared is sure to have been seen and questioned by one of these Constables which would certainly have "blown his cover." He would also have been an object of suspicion in the Hotel bar - a place not normally frequented by tramps.

The Mulberry Harbour Project

Three reinforced concrete caissons 200ft long, 45 ft wide and 24ft high, seen from the shorline in Rigg Bay. Each caisson weighed 3200 tons code name "Hippo". The steel spans were code named "Crocodile"

IWM

In Wigtownshire 1942 -1944

CHAPTER 2

With sections of two Royal Engineer Companies now installed in Garlieston and Cairnhead work on the three *Mulberry* schemes selected for trial commenced immediately.

THE HUGHES PIER

Iorys Hughes was a consulting engineer who had designed the Swimming Pool of Olympic standard built at Wembley in 1924 as part of the Empire Exhibition. His design consisted of a fixed pier and pierhead with two main component parts, large concrete caissons 200ft long and 45ft wide code named Hippo which would support steel spans code named Crocodile. The Hippos would be towed across the Channel to be sunk in position then the Crocodiles to be laid on top to form a roadway. Bruce White, now promoted to Brigadier rank, arranged construction of prototype caissons by Holloway Bros. Ltd., a large construction engineering firm. As no dry dock was available a site was found on a golf course at Conway, North Wales, adjacent to the tidal estuary of the River Conway. Three Hippo caissons each weighing 3200 tons were built here simultaneously. A steel superstructure was built on top of each caisson then they were launched sideways from a slipway, the largest craft then to have been lauched in this way. After launching in June and July 1943 the Hippos were towed to Rigg Bay, a mile south of Garlieston, where all three had arrived by early August. Two Crocodile units had arrived in Garlieston during June. By mid-August the Hippos had been positioned off-shore then, using the floating crane, linked by the Crocodiles.

The Mulberry Harbour Project

Swiss Roll section being unloaded from barge in Garlieston Harbour. 6 June 1943
IWM H30527

In Wigtownshire 1942 -1944

TN5 had by now realised that the potential of this scheme was considerably less than that shown by the two other schemes concurrently on trial so development and testing was stopped. The main disadvantage was that the pier could not rise and fall with the tide though adjustable approach spans to overcome this problem could have been produced had necessity so required. The Hippos had been found to have a liability to instability due to the scouring action of the tides washing around them which could have led to listing with possibly disastrous results.

The intention to bring a roadway ashore from the Hippos by placing Crocodiles on a series of caissons of diminishing size was not pursued, though before this decision was reached some preparations had been made. Sappers from 933 Company R.E. had built a solid stone base to hold the landward end of the innermost Crocodile just above high water mark in Rigg Bay. This was a tapered block 15 feet high by 25 feet wide with a maximum depth of 20 feet, built with dressed stone.

On 29th October, 1943 Hippo No.1, which had the largest superstructure, was towed to Garlieston where it was placed at the end of the harbour, thus providing additional mooring space and shelter for other equipment under test in the harbour.

SWISS ROLL

In 1940 the Admiralty formed the Royal Navy Directorate of Miscellaneous Weapon

The Mulberry Harbour Project

Aerial view of Swiss Roll at Cairnhead with an LCT attached. Spud Pier in background.
August 1943

IWM H32264

In Wigtownshire 1942 -1944

Development (DMWD) which brought together a group of Service and civilian scientists who in the following years of the war carried out research and development on a wide variety of ideas and inventions reaching them from many sources. In February 1942 DMWD heard of an inventor called Roland Marsden Hamilton who was experimenting in a small laboratory which he had constructed himself in a bomb damaged wing of the Grosvenor Hotel alongside London's Victoria Station. They found that Hamilton was a 42 year old with a crippled right arm which had prevented him from fulfilling his wish to serve in the Royal Navy in World War I. He was a brilliant mathematician who after gaining an Honours Degree at Oxford had spent several years working as a teacher in Public Schools. His flair for inventing, though hampered by lack of engineering training, had produced a flow of ideas most of which were not fully exploited due to his lack of capital and of business sense.

His crippled arm was a handicap but he was nevertheless an enthusiastic and capable yachtsman who had volunteered to assist in the evacuation of Dunkirk in May 1940. He joined the Ministry of Aircraft Production for a time, leaving them to work on his own on several ideas which he considered would be of value to the war effort including one which he had named "Rolling Dynamic Buoyancy". He was working on the development of this theory in the Grosvenor Hotel where he and his wife were living on their joint private incomes of about £300 per annum. He had been allowed by the owners of the Hotel to use space in an otherwise unoccupied bomb damaged wing.

Hamilton explained to DMWD that his theory was based on the Archimedean principles of

The Mulberry Harbour Project

Royal Engineer Diver about to make sea bed inspection of floating pier site. Tender *First* in background. March 1943

IWM H28115

In Wigtownshire 1942-1944

displacement before producing photographs of earlier experiments carried out with the assistance of his son Peter riding a motor cycle, with a pillion passenger, across a wide stream supported only by chestnut fencing stakes laid over a tarpaulin. He proceeded to explain the experiments he was then carrying out in the Hotel. He had built a 200ft long tank from old linoleum and bricks in a corridor filling it with a hose from the bathroom tap. Floating in the tank was a minature roadway made of strips of wood and canvas anchored by wires fore and aft. As a model truck ran across this roadway, hinged sides turned up to prevent water flowing over, then dropped level as the truck passed. According to his calculations a full scale floating roadway constructed of Douglas fir planking joined by flexible steel cables would carry a 10 ton vehicle over water for a distance of one mile.

Hamilton was immediately taken on the strength of DMWD as a consultant engineer with a brief to develop his floating bridge to which DMWD gave the codename Swiss Roll from the intention to roll sections on a spindle for transportation. In the event full scale sections, when rolled, looked exactly like a huge, if inedible, Swiss Roll.

By June 1942 a full scale length, built with planking lined with water-proof canvas had been constructed in Portsmouth to be placed on trial in the Dockyard there. Mr and Mrs Hamilton moved to Portsmouth where they were joined by Peter who worked with his father for long hours throughout every possible break from his studies for Cambridge University entrance. Many problems which arose were overcome, for instance Ronald Hamilton designed an ingenious kerb system which allowed vehicles to use the roadway safely in complete darkness. Stability tests were carried out by

The Mulberry Harbour Project

Two Swiss Roll sections unrolled in Garlieston Harbour alongside Crocodiles 1 and 2. Swiss Roll barges in foreground. Concrete Beetles on left. 23 June 1943

IWM H30937

bringing a motor torpedo boat into the dockyard basin to deliberately raise seven foot waves whilst a lorry was driven along the track. This resulted in a report that "the bridge will be unharmed by storms and will be usable in all but the worst weather."

During the period of these trials, Hamilton was difficult to work with, he was working under considerable stress and he was a perfectionist who continually found need for improvement. He envisaged possible, even if improbable, snags and mishaps to which he sought solutions, working long hours without a break or relaxation.

At the end of 1942 the tests in Portsmouth were concluded with a decision to carry out further tests in the open sea. Arrangements were made to construct further sections of Swiss Roll in Bute West Docks, Cardiff. The intention was to carry out sea trials at Appledore in Devon but early in 1943 responsibility passed from DMWD to TN5 with the result that all further tests were in Wigtown Bay.

A Garlieston resident whose house overlooks the habour has recounted how he awoke early one summer morning in 1943. He was aware that it was high water and whilst he could see the pier, the surface of the water was not in his view. To his amazement he could see several soldiers apparently walking across the harbour with ease where he knew there was at least 10 feet of water! He was quickly out of bed to find out that they were walking on a length of what he now knows was Swiss Roll. Several rolls each some 200ft long, had arrived from Cardiff in barges and the first roll had

The Mulberry Harbour Project

Loaded 3 ton Thorneycroft Tipper Truck left to stand on Swiss Roll in floatation test. 22 inches of water on surface after 26 minutes. 5 August 1943

IWM H31612

been unloaded then towed out across the harbour early this morning. The date was 6th June, 1943, exactly one year before the invasion of Europe was to commence. During the next week or so more rolls were unloaded then unrolled in the harbour, to be towed to Cairnhead where a stretch of shoreline had been prepared with a roadway leading down to high water mark. These rolls were linked together to form a floating roadway some 1500ft long with the seaward end attached to mooring buoys. A series of tests then commenced with Ronald and Peter Hamilton arriving early in July to participate. Ronald Hamilton had calculated mathematically that a loaded vehicle standing on the roadway would stay afloat for three hours. This theory was put to test in his presence on 5th August when practice disproved theory. In a moderate sea a loaded 3 ton Thorneycroft tipper truck sank in just over 90 minutes. No pierhead was used in these trials, instead trials were carried out in linking a Tank Landing Craft ramp directly to the Swiss Roll then driving vehicles off.

The series of tests carried out in the open sea showed that the earlier, more limited, tests in the dockyard could not be wholly relied upon. It was found that the heaviest load which could be carried was 7 tons which ruled out bringing tanks ashore. Trucks had to be driven slowly in second gear with the result that engines frequently overheated. Swiss Roll had not, despite Portsmouth conclusions, behaved well in heavy seas. TN5 conclusions were that despite advantages of cheap and easy manufacture, Swiss Roll would not be suitable for *Mulberry* purposes.

Mention should be made of another Ronald Hamilton invention which he had purposed to use as a pierhead with Swiss Roll. This was a flexible floating carpet made up from hexagonal

The Mulberry Harbour Project

Foreground right to left: Major Carline, Brigadier Bruce White, Ronald Hamilton, Peter Hamilton at Cairnhead. 9 July 1943

IWM H31283

buoyancy tanks 6 feet wide and 30 inches deep which could be linked together to form any required shape and size whilst retaining a surface rigid enough to carry heavy weights. His original idea had been to use this as a floating runway for aircraft. DMWD had given this invention the code name Lily from the similarity in appearance of the units to a giant water lily.

Full scale trials were held in the Clyde, south of the Isle of Arran, where it was found that an airstrip 600 feet by 60 feet could be assembled in one hour. From this small strip Swordfish and Auster aircraft successfully landed and took off, pilots reporting little difference from aircraft carrier operations. These floating airstrips were considered to have tremendous potential for use in the Far East in the war against Japan but, before they could be produced, the Hiroshima atom bomb attack effectively ended the Far East conflict.

A number of Lily units were taken to Garlieston but they were not tried out with Swiss Roll.

THE TN5 PIER

The design conceived and sponsored by TN5 was for a floating road bridge linked to a floating pier. The bridge was designed by W.T. Everall a railway engineer who had come home from India at the outbreak of war to join the War Office. He was appointed as Chief Bridging Instructor at an Army Railway Training Centre where a flexible gangway he had designed to enable railway locomotives to be loaded and unloaded from ferry steamers became the basis of his bridge design.

The Mulberry Harbour Project

Concrete Beetle in Garlieston Harbour. LCT238 in background. March 1943

IWM H28098

In Wigtownshire 1942 -1944

The design used floating pontoons to carry steel spans which could be assembled to any required length. To meet the load requirement of 56 tons per float, Everall's design was for a steel float 42ft long by 15ft wide weighing 16 tons. Estimates were that 460 floats would eventually be needed which would require over 7000 tons of steel in addition to the requirements for pierheads and bridging. As such demands were impossible to meet due to other wartime needs it was decided to make floats from concrete which was of course returning to Winston Churchill's 1917 suggestion.

Concrete vessels in a variety of sizes had been built and used in small numbers since World War I but there were no established builders. Wates Ltd, Construction Engineers, working in Vickers Shipyard at Barrow-in-Furness were requested to produce designs and in due course they produced floats weighing 46 tons with similar dimensions to the steel floats. They were fitted with wooden fenders to protect sides and bottom and they fully met Everall's requirements. A design feature of steel and concrete floats was the turtleback shape which reduced the tendency to pitch when afloat and gave origin to the codename Beetle.

Steel spans 80ft long by 10ft wide were constructed by an engineering firm, Braithwaites Ltd in West Bromwich. They included a telescopic span fitted with a simple sliding panel device which allowed adjustments in span length between 71ft and 80ft to allow for expansion and contraction caused by rising and falling tides. It was calculated that one such span included in each five spans would absorb the variations in length of a bridge one mile long. Most of the span components were welded rather than riveted, this comparatively new technique saved many tons of steel.

The Mulberry Harbour Project

Tow with wooden fairing fitted to beam of leading Beetle leaving Garlieston Bay.
March 1944

IWM H36515

In Wigtownshire 1942 -1944

The pierhead for the TN5 design was based on a dredger built at Renfrew in 1923 by Lobnitz & Co. Ltd for work in the Bahamas. To keep her stable this vessel was fitted with three legs with splay feet called spuds which could be embedded in the sea bottom and on which she could ride up and down with the tides. Bruce White consulted Henry Lobnitz who was quickly able to adapt his dredger design to a large steel pontoon. This rectangular pontoon was 200ft long by 60ft wide with four high stacks, one on each corner, holding spud legs 89ft long with feet 4ft square. These legs could be driven up and down whilst retaining lateral rigidity. Generators were fitted to power two 20hp electric motors to drive the spuds which could be operated individually to allow for uneven surface of the seabed. Accommodation for a crew of 22 was provided and total weight was 1100 tons. Construction of a prototype was carried out by Alex Findlay & Co. Ltd of Motherwell who had taken over a derelict shipyard at Old Kilpatrick on the Clyde.

As has already been said, 167 Company, Royal Engineers were engaged on bridge erection trials near to the Vickers Yard at Barrow where the beetles were being built when they were ordered to Cairnhead. Their War Diary shows that work started immediately on arrival to build a conventional Army design landward approach, twelve bays of "V Trestling Pier Approach" having been erected by 12th March, 1943. This approach was to be used by the TN5 pier.

Meantime concrete beetles were arriving in Garlieston from Barrow together with component parts of several steel beetles, which were bolted together in the harbour to form complete units. These steel beetles were used on the landward span of the pier shortly to be erected at Cairnhead as

The Mulberry Harbour Project

Aerial view of Hippo 1 in position at Garlieston harbour. 7 November 1943.

IWM H34514

concrete beetles proved to be subject to damage from continual grounding at each tide. Six steel bridge spans arrived in Garlieston by LCT from Barrow during March.

Progress reports made by Captain D.J. Tonks of 167 Company state that work to place the spans on beetles commenced on 12th March and continued until the end of the month hampered at times by severe weather conditions. The spans were hoisted in pairs, one above the other, on to two beetles placed abreast, then towed to Cairnhead where the top span was slid forward on to another beetle to form a two span unit. This method proved to be unsuitable as the erection teams found it difficult to control the movement of the spans. After experiment the difficulties were overcome by moving the spans individually using an erection tank. This was a long welded steel cylinder 8ft in diameter with conical ends which, when filled with compressed air, carried one end of a span when on tow. When the span was in position over a beetle the tank was flooded and removed then trumpet shaped guides enabled adjacent spans to be rapidly linked.

The method of mooring the roadway, particularly the racking (i.e. sideways) movement, presented problems. A self burying kite anchor weighing only 6cwt which would take a pull of some 20 tons was developed. Two of these anchors were carried in a raft, or shuttle, which had a drum holding 1200 feet of mooring wire. This shuttle was carried on a span until required, then launched, to be taken in tow by a shallow draught motor boat which had been designed by yacht builders Camper & Nicholson Ltd and was known as a surf landing under girder, or slug boat. When launched the shuttle cast an anchor 600 feet upstream from a beetle then proceeded, paying

The Mulberry Harbour Project

Spud Pontoon no. 13 under construction on a slipway at Cairnryan. February 1944
IWM H35937

out mooring wire attached to the anchor, passing under the floating roadway to cast the second anchor 600 feet downstream. The mooring cable was made fast to the beetle by cable stoppers then hauled in to the required tension by a "pull lift" device. Trials showed that this anchor laying operation could be completed in comparatively short time. The slug boats which were 20 feet long were manned by a crew of two. They carried a winch and a compressor used to fill Erection Tanks. They were fitted with a steel grill all round the edge which protected the crew from decapitation when passing under the bridge!

The spud pontoon christened "Winnie" by her builders, who had completed her in the remarkably short time of four months, was launched on 8th April; then arrived at Cairnhead under tow on 22th April. Due to unfavourable weather she was allowed to stand on her spud legs until 27th April before being connected to the pier. Some three weeks later the complete pier underwent its first spell of severe weather. In winds gusting up to 60 mph with waves rising from 6 to 12 feet a visiting drifter from 467 Motor Boat Company RASC was driven ashore and severely damaged with the crew being rescued with nothing worse than a thorough wetting. Apart from a few loosened bolts in the decking of the roadway, the pier suffered no damage.

BREAKWATERS

A paper presented to the Institute of Civil Engineers in 1945 by Major A.H. Beckett, RE, who had been a member of the TN 5 team, stated "Trials with *Mulberry* floating roadways were carried

The Mulberry Harbour Project

Hippo no. 2 under tow from Conway to Rigg Bay. 5 August 1943

IWM H31617

out on an exposed coast in South West Scotland where a six span pontoon bridge was installed. No breakwater was provided."

However, sheltered water was an essential part of the *Mulberry* scheme which required the provision of breakwaters on a substantial scale. A great deal of experiment and trial was undertaken, principally by DMWD, before reaching a decision that the breakwater around each *Mulberry* should consist of three elements. These were firstly no less than 59 obsolete merchant and naval vessels to be sunk as an outer line, these vessels began to assemble off Oban in April 1944 to be stripped, ballasted and fittted with explosive charges, to later proceed under their own steam to be sunk in the required position. This outer line was codenamed *Gooseberry*. The second line was to be formed by concrete caissons codenamed *Phoenix*. It was estimated that at least 200 caissons would be required with a total length exceeding 20,000 feet of which 10,000 feet would have to be 60 feet high. Design and construction experience gained on the Hippos proved to be invaluable in the subsequent construction of *Phoenix* caissons. Finally, there would be a floating breakwater, codenamed *Bombardon*, constructed from steel sections in cruciform shape which had been designed and developed by DMWD engineers.

During the period from March to July 1943 TN 5 were in close touch with all that was going on in Wigtown Bay. Brigadier Bruce White and several of his senior aides - Lt. Colonel J.R. Sainsbury, Major Steer Webster and others - were regular visitors to Garlieston and Cairnhead and many of the problems arising were taken back to the engineering team at TN 5 H.Q. for solution. By late July

The Mulberry Harbour Project

Crusader tank travelling at 30mph on floating pier. August 1943

IWM H30929

In Wigtownshire 1942 -1944

TN 5 had decided that the spud pontoon with its floating pier should be the scheme they would recommend for *Mulberry* use.

Several parties of senior officers from the Admiralty, the War office and from Allied Forces visited to see for themselves the progress being made. As early as 13th March, Major General Sir Riddle Webster, the Quartermaster General, visited with members of his staff whilst on 23rd June a party of Naval and Army senior officers including Major General C.J.S. King, the Engineer-in-Chief, and Major General D.J. McMullen, War Office Director of Transportation, watched a demonstration of the capabilities of the spud pontoon and pier at Cairnhead. Crusader tanks weighing 20 tons, tank transporters and other vehicles were unloaded from a vessel moored alongside then driven over the bridge at up to 40 mph. Even with a calm sea the spectators were impressed.

Other regular visitors between March 1943 and April 1944 were photographers from the Army Film and Photographic Unit. Several hundred photographs of all aspects of *Mulberry* construction and use are now held by the Imperial War Museum in London. Their records show that during March and April 1943 many of the Wigtown Bay photographs were taken by Sgt. A. Hardy, using the standard Army issue camera - a German made Super Ikonta! Sgt. Hardy is better known as Bert Hardy, for many years Chief Photographer with Picture Post. Before he joined the Army his photographs, taken on the night of 11th January, 1941, of firemen working in London at the height of the blitz, were published around the world and he was later to win many awards for photographs taken during the Korean War. In his autobiography published in 1985 he writes "None of the

The Mulberry Harbour Project

Tugs **Ajay** and **Ebro** towing spans after salvage from Eggerness Point with an erection tank replacing damaged Beetle. 27 February 1944

IWM H36338

In Wigtownshire 1942 -1944

photographic jobs I was given to do by the Army at this time was very interesting. I spent more than a month on the West Coast of Scotland taking pictures of the construction of a *Mulberry* harbour, a prefabricated metal platform floating on barge-like bases. The camp seemed to be in the middle of no-where." The camp to which he refers is Cairnhead.

The Mulberry Harbour Project

Aerial view of Hippos in Rigg Bay with both crocodiles in place.
August 1943

IWM H32263

In Wigtownshire 1942 -1944

CHAPTER 3

On the 4th August 1943 Winston Churchill sailed from the Clyde aboard the Queen Mary en route for a Conference with President Roosevelt in Quebec.

British and American planning staffs working on "Overlord", as the invasion of Europe had been codenamed, attended this Conference which commenced on 14 August. After Prime Minister Churchill had arrived, the War Office were requested to send a team conversant with *Mulberry* to Quebec as a matter of urgency. General Sir Harold Wernher who had recently been appointed *Mulberry* co-ordinator, with Brigadier Bruce White and Major Steer Webster of TN 5, together with five DMWD scientists, was hastily assembled. They flew out from Prestwick seated on palliasses in the bomb bay of a Liberator bomber, reaching Montreal via Newfoundland after an extremely uncomfortable 18 hour journey. At Montreal they transferred to a Dakota to complete the journey to Quebec where their first meeting in the Chateau Frontenac started less than an hour after their arrival.

The floating pier concept was completely novel to the Americans but, after some explanation, the idea was enthusiastically accepted. Over the following three weeks a great deal of hard work was put in by Wernher's team, first in Quebec then in Washington. Meetings and conferences with British and American members of the Overlord staff continued for twelve to fifteen hours every day examining all aspects of *Mulberry* - logistics, design, construction, etc etc. Agreement was reached

The Mulberry Harbour Project

Rigg Bay. 11th March 1944

IWM H36532

In Wigtownshire 1942 -1944

that the Overlord plan should include two artificial harbours, *Mulberry* A to be used by American Forces and *Mulberry* B to be used by British Forces. Hours after the final sessions ended Wernher's team were over the Atlantic flying home.

A great deal remained to be done in the time now remaining, with the projected invasion date only months ahead. Orders were placed for the construction of four miles of floating pier and six spud pierheads and work quickly started on sites all over Britian. Eventually 22 spud pontoons and ten miles of floating pier was built. With construction capacity already stretched to its limits it was necessary to find many new sites and to train workers in new skills. The Ministry of Supply set up mobile teams who went to many sites to train tailors, hairdressers and many others in the then comparatively new techniques of welding. 13 complete spud pontoons were built at Leith, the first being launched on 20 January 1944. Five more were built at Morfa near Conway, close to the original Hippo site, where 900 men and women worked day and night ignoring blackout regulations. The remaining four pontoons were built on a slipway just north of No.2 Military Port, Cairnryan, the first three by Royal Engineer Sappers and the fourth by civilians sent from Leith.

The pontoons built at Morfa and at Cairnryan were towed to Southampton where the spud columns and legs were fitted by Dorman Long Ltd. All of the spud pontoon construction was under the overall control of Alex Findlay & Co. Ltd who had built the prototype. In addition to the spud pontoons, 20 intermediate pontoons were also built, 90 feet long, they were to be inserted between the spud pontoons to extend the pierhead length. The extended pierheads were given the codename *Whale*.

The Mulberry Harbour Project

Another major concern was the construction within the time limits of the caissons needed for the Phoenix breakwater. 210 were required in six types ranging in size from 1672 tons to 6044 tons. Every possible dry dock was brought into use and, in addition, a number of makeshift docks were constructed on the estuaries of the Thames, Clyde and other rivers where caissons could be partially constructed before floating out for completion alongside a quay. One of the sites utilised was the East India Dock in Poplar, London. When the dock was drained in December 1943 for the first time since construction in the early 1800's the dock walls collapsed creating a considerable reconstruction task for the Port of London Authority. Three of the larger caissons, each 200 feet long by 60 feet high, which had been built on the Clyde were "parked" close inshore in Rigg Bay for several weeks before being towed to an assembly point on the South Coast close to Selsey Bill. A local resident described them as each being as large as a block of flats.

Steel beetles were assembled at Richborough in Kent from components brought in from factories around the country, then spans also assembled on site, were added. Concrete beetles were constructed behind hoardings on the seafront at Southsea and at Marchwood, Southampton, on a site now occupied by a large power station. Spans were added in Southampton Water. Much of this work was undertaken by Sappers who would later by involved in erecting *Mulberry* on the invasion beaches.

Throughout the Autumn of 1943 and into the Spring of 1944, tests and trials continued in Wigtown Bay concentrating now on the TN 5 floating pier. Clearly the conventional pier approach

In Wigtownshire 1942 -1944

which had been erected at Cairnhead would not be feasible on an invasion beach. A steel shore ramp was designed which had a shoreward height of six inches and a seaward end seven feet high to which a span could be attached. This ramp could be beached then, with the floating pier attached, vehicles could be driven straight off. The ramp was fitted with two sets of davits each of which would carry a slug boat. Beaching trials were carried out between January and March 1944 in Rigg Bay before a total of eight ramps were built, four for each *Mulberry*.

The Admiralty advised that LCT required to berth bow on to unload and that LST, which carried up to 50 vehicles, could unload more rapidly if berthed bow on with top and main decks discharging simultaneously. A wedge-shaped buffer pontoon with the thick end hinged to the spud pontoon was designed and built. This enabled an LCT to run up, effectively beaching on the buffer, then drop her bow door straight on to the deck of the spud pontoon. A high level ramp built from Bailey Bridge components on the deck of the spud pontoon enabled an LST berthing on the buffer pontoon to fully unload both decks in 15 to 20 minutes.

It was intended to tow the pier across the Channel in six span units which would be almost 500 feet long. As it was important to know how such tows would behave in various sea conditions, a series of trials was conducted in Wigtown Bay. A six span unit was towed by the tug **Ebro** along a measured mile marked by bouys. In an early test in heavy seas during January 1944 a tow was lost when a rope broke, apparently due to the advise of Captain Jansma not being accepted. All six spans went aground on rocks close to Eggerness Point where they remained until salvaged in calm weather at the end of February. Erection tanks proved to be invaluable in the salvage operations. Two concrete beetles which suffered some damage were left on the rocks.

In an endeavour to reduce the towing load by streamlining a wooden fairing was built on to the beam of the leading beetle in a tow. This was tested in March 1944 but was abandoned mainly because a quick release, intended to drop the fairing when no longer required, could not be made to work properly. It is understood that a later model was a success.

Most of the trials had been completed by the end of March 1944 which allowed efforts to be concentrated on the already commenced training of troops who would install and operate the *Mulberry*s on the invasion beaches. In a lecture given at Imperial College, London, on 17 June 1975, Mr R.J.P. Cowan described how, early in 1944, the War Office set about organising the assembly of the men to be trained. He was then a young engineering graduate of Glasgow University serving with the Royal Engineers in the Middle East. With a number of other young Officers, he reported as instructed to the War Office where they were told that they would be trained in "Supervision and Control of Harbour Installation" at Cairnhead, then assist in the training of sappers. They were advised that the War Office had sent an Order to all Royal Engineer Units in the United Kingdom requiring that batches of "the best men in the Unit" were to be sent to Cairnhead for an unspecified task. Inevitably the Units receiving this Order took the opportunity to get rid of the men they did not want! Captain Gearge Tarling, a Regular Royal Engineer, duly received these men at Glasserton House, some five miles from Cairnhead, which had been requisitioned to accommodate

In Wigtownshire 1942 -1944

the trainees. Many arrived with army crime sheets listing offences ranging from insubordination, drunkeness, theft and absence without leave to more serious offences. Though kept hard at work they still found time for mischief, several men were charged with setting fire to Glasserton House, fortunately the fire was quickly detected and no serious damage resulted. From the point of view of the owner the greater damage was probably that caused by the men who, unable to force the door padlocks, obtained entry to the wine cellar by digging through the kitchen floor then drinking wines which in wartime were irreplaceable! They too were apprehended and charged, at the end of May 1944 Captain Tarling was reported to have twenty-two Courts Martial pending! In fairness Mr Cowan added that Captain Tarling and other instructors did succeed in their tasks as, in the event, the trainees did a magnificent job on the invasion beaches. As each batch of men completed their training at Cairnhead they were despatched to one of the Units at Richborough or Marchwood where they worked on beetle and bridge span assembly until just before the invasion commenced. In addition to sappers, a large number of sailors from United States Navy Construction Battalions (The Seabees), who would be responsible for the erection of *Mulberry* A for the US Forces, were trained at Cairnhead. These sailors were accommodated at RAF Station, Wigtown travelling to and from Cairnhead daily. The US Navy uniform with distinctive "Seabee" shoulder flash became a familiar sight in public houses in Wigtown and Newton Stewart where the reason for the presence of US sailors on an airfield in Wigtownshire was the subject of much speculation. No doubt the sailors had some knowledge of the reasons but security was not breached.

The Mulberry Harbour Project

CHAPTER 4

In the Spring and early Summer of 1944 beetles, bombardons, phoenix caissons, whales and the many other items comprising the component parts of *Mulberry* -a total of almost one and a half million tons for both harbours- were brought to assembly points spread along the south coast from Pegwell Bay in Kent to Selsey in Dorset in preparation for the tow of around 100 miles to the chosen *Mulberry* sites. *Mulberry* B was destined to be erected at Arromanches-Les-Bains, a Normandy village described as standing on a shallow bay on the Calvados coastline with cliffs on either side.

When on D-Day, 6 June 1944, the invasion of Europe commenced, the movement of *Mulberry* Units started at once. The gooseberry blockships for *Mulberry* B at Arromanches were in position by D+4 (that is 4 days after D-Day), and the phoenix caissons followed immediately. By 9 June erection of piers had started and on 14 June the first spud pontoon was attached allowing coasters to start discharging 3 ton lorries. The harbour was completed by 7 June despite many setbacks occasioned by unfavourable weather and other hazards. The greater part of *Mulberry* B construction was undertaken by sappers trained at Cairnhead together with many of those who had been at Wigtown Bay from the beginning of the exercise, including Lt. Colonel Carline and Lt. Colonel Tonks, both now promoted. 2000 feet of swiss roll, all brought from Cairnhead, was laid at Arromanches where it was used by the Royal Navy to disembark Royal Marines and other troops. After a visit to *Mulberry* B on 23 July Winton Churchill signalled to the Naval Officer in Charge

In Wigtownshire 1942 -1944

"this miraculous port has played and will continue to play a most important part in the liberation of Europe." First news of the harbours was given to the general public on 22 September when press releases said that "two harbours each the size of Gibraltar Harbour have been built on the enemy coastline." A later and probably more accurate assessment described *Mulberry* B as "containing 1300 acres which is approximately the size of Dover Harbour". By the end of October 1944 *Mulberry* B had landed 627,719 tons of supplies, 39,743 vehicles and many thousands of men.

There can be no doubt that *Mulberry* played a decisive part in the success of the invasion of Europe and there can equally be no doubt that eighteen months of hard work in and around Wigtown Bay played a decisive part in the success of *Mulberry*.

In 1945 a paper produced for the Cabinet Office by Captain G.R.G. Allen, Royal Navy, estimated the total cost of the *Mulberry* project as being in the order of twenty million pounds and that 40,000 men had been involved at the peak of production.

In March 1945 BBC radio broadcast a ninety minute documentary titled "The Harbour called *Mulberry*" which had a distinguished cast including Valentine Dyall and Arnold Ridley. The Radio Critic of "The Observer", W.E. Williams, suggested that "this wireless epic" should be broadcast in the USA and translations broadcast in Russia and France as it "vividly and faithfully revealed the British war effort". He also commented that "No other nation than ours would contrive such an impudent solution to its problem of invasion than to take its own harbour along".

The Mulberry Harbour Project

CHAPTER 5

At the end of 1944 Brigadier Bruce White was appointed Knight Commander of the British Empire, an honour which he considered recognised the entire TN 5 team which, in addition to *Mulberry*, had been responsible for the planning and construction of No.1 Military Port at Faslane on the Clyde and No.2 Military Port at Cairnryan. After the war ended he became Senior Partner in a firm of Consulting Engineers, Sir Bruce White, Wolfe, Barry & Partners which remained in business until the mid-1980's.

Ronald Hamilton had his patents for Swiss Roll and Lily returned to him soon after the war ended and he was given an award of £8,000 for his wartime inventions. He formed a company to exploit Lily but several ambitious plans had not matured when he died in January 1953.

Captain Jansma of **Ebro** returned to Holland before emigrating to Australia.

At Garlieston and Cairnhead virtually all Swiss Roll and Spud pier equipment had been taken away before the end of May 1944 to be used at Arromanches. Hippo No.1 remained in Garlieston harbour until, at the request of the Harbour Committee, it was towed back to Rigg Bay to join the two others which remain there. Eventually the steel superstructure on two hippos was dismantled and they were taken to Larne to be used in harbour construction work. The third hippo which had suffered damage to the base was not considered to be suitable for re-use. Now in 1993 it still stands

In Wigtownshire 1942 -1944

in Rigg Bay almost 50 years after launching at Conway though viewed from close quarters in Autumn 1992 the steel superstructure shows clear indications of deterioration. On the shoreline, the stone crocodile terminal remains intact. Also still to be seen are two beetles lying on rocks close to Eggerness Point where they were left when damaged in January 1944. Survival of over 48 years of Solway tides and storms pays tribute to the original design and construction of hippo and beetle and to the craftsmanship of the R.E. stonemasons.

The Mulberry Harbour Project

GLOSSARY

(i) ABBREVIATIONS

DMWD	Department of Miscellaneous Weapon Development (Admiralty)
LCT	Landing Craft Tank
LST	Landing Ship Tank
MOWT	Ministry of War and Transport
RASC	Royal Army Service Corps
RE	Royal Engineers
TN 5	Transportation 5, Directorate of Transport, War Office

(ii) CODENAMES

BEETLE	Reinforced Concrete, or Steel, Pontoon to carry floating roadway
BOMBARDON	Floating Steel Breakwater
CROCODILE	Steel span for Hughes Pier
ERECTION TANK	Cylindrical Steel Tank used for connecting roadway spans
GOOSEBERRY	Breakwater formed by sunken ships
HIPPO	Concrete Caisson for Hughes Pier
MULBERRY	Artificial Harbour

In Wigtownshire 1942 -1944

OVERLORD	Invasion of Europe Plan
PHOENIX	Concrete Caissons for Breakwater
SHORE RAMP	Wedge shaped float connecting floating bridge to shore
SLUG BOAT	Boat used with mooring floats to anchor Beetles
SPUD PONTOON	Floating pierhead with four legs embedded in sea bottom
SWISS ROLL	Floating timber roadway
WHALE	Floating pierhead

(iii) SHIPPING

EBRO   Steel Tug Built Rotterdam 1931. Home port Rotterdam. 108 H.P. (Lloyds Register 1938)

LCT   Large numbers of Landing Craft Tank ranging in size from 30 tons to 300 tons were built in the United Kingdom and USA. Those used to transport materials to Garlieston (No.'s 238, 270 and 273) were of medium size; No. 484 used with Swiss Roll at Cairnhead was of 300 tons, 171 feet long by 39 feet.

LST   400 Landing Ship Tanks were built in USA in 1942/43 for supply to Great Britain on a wartime lend-lease agreement. They had a capacity of 2500 tons and held up to 50 vehicles. 14 were lost by enemy action, the remainder were returned to USA in 1945/47.

The Mulberry Harbour Project

No record of Tug *Ajay* can be traced. An immediate post-war edition of "British Tugs" by Ian Allen Ltd points out that with 8000 Barges in use on the Thames, their listing of Thames Tugs is not comprehensive as it omits small tugs operated by smaller companies.

In Wigtownshire 1942 -1944

ACKNOWLEDGMENTS

Crown Copyright material in the Public Records Office is reproduced by permission of the Controller of Her Majesty's Stationery Office.
Documents consulted were:
        WO 166/12073
        CAB 101/236
        CAB 106/968

The photographs are reproduced by the courtesy of the Imperial War Museum.

The Local History Series

This series of books is being published in order to satisfy the ever increasing interest in the history of Galloway, especially the county of Wigtownshire. It is our intention to continue to publish further titles indefinitely as and when they are ready for printing. Some of the books will be previously unpublished material. As such they will be in great demand by local historians, educationalists and libraries along with the "man in the street".

No 1	"Pigot's Directory of Wigtownshire 1837"	£3.00
No 4	"The Mulberry Harbour Project in Wigtownshire" 2nd ed.	£5.95
No 5	"Pigot's Directory of Kirkcudbrightshire 1837"	£3.00
No 6	"Pigot's Directory of Dumfriesshire 1837"	£4.50
No 7	"Pigot's Directory of Ayrshire 1837"	£6.50
No 8	"Albanich - The History of the Galloway Rifles"	£28.50
No 9	"History of Sorbie Parish Church"	£3.00
No 12	"Ruby - Life in Galloway & Glasgow"	£3.00
No 13	"Lands & Their Owners in Galloway" 5 vols., 2500pp hd. bk. in cloth	£100.00
No 14	"Highways & Byways in Galloway"	Out of print
No 15	"The Persecutions in Scotland, 1605 - 1685"	£4.00
No 16	"Reminiscences of Wigtonshire" Samuel Robinson	£10.95
No 17	"A Sailor Boy's Experience" Samuel Robinson	£12.95
No 18	"The Lost Railways of Galloway"	£4.00
No 20	"The Lost Railways of Ayrshire"	£5.95
No 21	"Cairn Ryan Military Port - A History"	£6.95
No 22	"Penninghame - The Story of a Parish"	£16.95
No 23	"Exploring Galloway - A Series of Sixteen Historical Walks"	£6.45
No 24	"RAF in Galloway" second edition	available Autumn '99
No 25	"William Nicholson - The Bard of Galloway"	£6.95
No 26	"The House that Sugar Built"	available Summer '99